Print Vol. I No. 1, June 1940

Howard Trafton (cover designer)

Bruce Rogers (thumbprints contributor)

H oward Trafton (1897–1964) designed the first *Print* cover, and the reason for that is not entirely clear. But Trafton, who taught at The Art Students League of New York and is best known for the typefaces Trafton Script (1933) and Cartoon (1936), believed that the principles of art and design were the same. It was daring for *Print* to publish such an abstract cover (even though the thumbprints belonged to the classical book designer Bruce Rogers). In a way, this cover illustrated a footnote to the first editorial, which read, "There has been little agreement so far as to a proper definition of the term 'graphic arts.' *Print* takes the term broadly: to describe all the means by which ideas are reproduced in visual form."

print

Vol. II · No 1

A quarterly Journal of the graphic Arts

METZIG

Print Vol. II No. 1, May/June 1941

William Metzig (cover designer)

William Edwin Rudge established *Print* to advocate a masterful level of craft and precision. German-born William Metzig (1893–1989) met those expectations with his design of this calligraphic cover, which was produced before *Print* settled on a fixed nameplate. Metzig founded a design and lettering studio in Hanover, Germany, during the 1920s, where he designed trademarks, logos, letterheads, brochures and posters, notably for the Pelikan Ink Company. A leading calligrapher in Germany, he transplanted well when he immigrated to the U.S. in 1939 and settled in New York. There, he taught his exemplary style while carrying out assignments and writing the book *Heraldry for the Designer* (1983).

Print Vol. V No. 4, 1948

Imre Reiner (cover artist)

The handlettered exuberance of Imre Reiner (1900-1987), a Hungarian-born type designer and author of books on type and lettering, stands out among *Print*'s early covers, and many of the later covers, for being robust and joyful. The fungible nature of the *Print* nameplate did not restrict designers like Reiner, who took full ownership of the space to exercise his lettering muscles. This form of illustrated typography fell out of favor when modernism kicked in during the early 1950s—indeed, extreme lettering like this was not seen again for decades, although today the aesthetic and practice are back in force. Reiner wrote now-classic books, such as *Modern and Historical Typography* (1946), that promoted a range of modern and eclectic lettering. He also designed many typefaces, including Meridian (1930), Corvinus (1934), Matura (1938), Mercurius Script (1957) and Pepita (1959).

Print

IX:4

Print IX:4, 1955

Jerome Snyder (cover artist)

S till with William Edwin Rudge Publisher Inc., *Print*'s format moved from that of essentially a journal to a magazine. While retaining much of the same content as earlier volumes, including a feature on figurative typography, the magazine also stepped outside of the norms with an article on printmaker Josef Scharl by the Albert Einstein. This cover, by *Sports Illustrated* art director and illustrator Jerome Snyder (1916–1976), stretched around to the back and offered a little cognitive dissonance from the articles on classical themes, instead illustrating the variety of entries in the AIGA's 13th Annual Exhibition of Design and Printing for Commerce. Snyder later co-authored with Milton Glaser a popular column in *New York Magazine* called The Underground Gourmet.

Print

ITALIAN ISSUE X:2

Print X:2, April/May 1956

Leo Lionni (cover artist)

With a new magazine format, *Print* turned to Dutch-born, Italian-adopted, New York–based co-editor Leo Lionni (1910-1999) to design a distinctive nameplate from a typeface called Chisel. Lionni also contributed a column titled The Lion's Tail, which featured visual phenomena from past and present. His cover for the special Italian Issue was inspired by a Ravenna floor mosaic. The issue featured stories on the etchings of Giorgio Morandi, the editorial art of *Domus* magazine and a parable about a beautiful graffiti-covered wall in the Murano islands near Venice. The Lionni hand and eye was all over this issue.

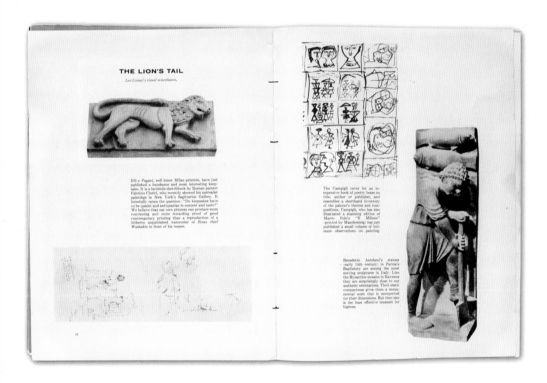

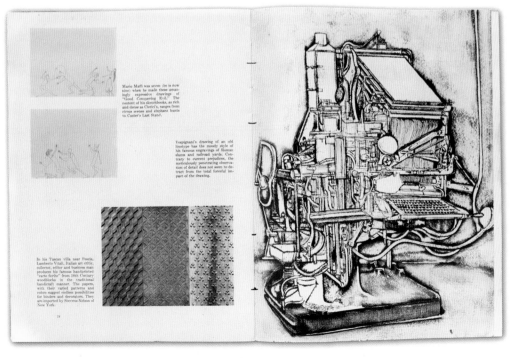

Print

X:3

Print X:3, June/July 1956

No credit information cited

This issue of *Print* featured a story on experiments in visual perception titled "Transaction Design," which today signifies an entirely new world of cross-disciplinary practice. The cover, however, was a high-contrast picture of the walls of the New York City subway. The editorial note stated that this chaotic clutter was "an ever-present challenge to anyone with a message, a knife, a pencil or even a lipstick." Presumably, the cover tied tacitly into the feature "Circles in the Square" about the design of manhole covers. The description of this article read: "Cast iron beauty and design underfoot."

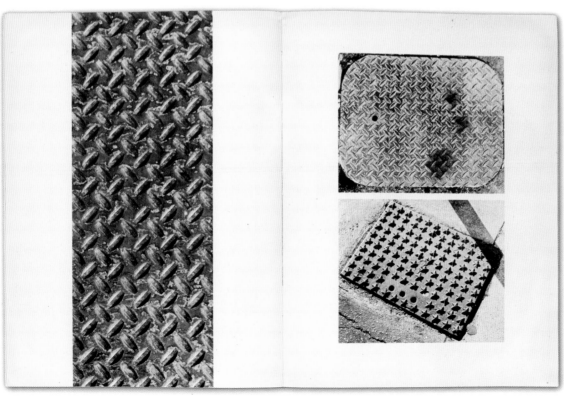

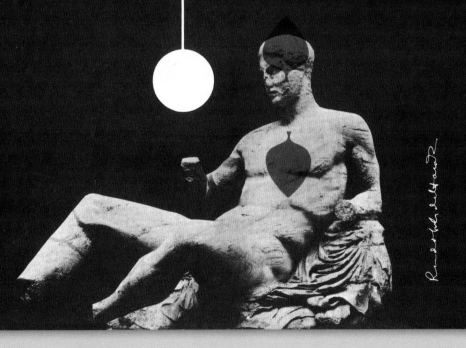

Print XI:3

Print XI:3, 1957

Rudolph de Harak (cover artist)

B y this issue, Leo Lionni's name no longer appeared on the mast-
head, The Lion's Tail was gone and, interestingly, a memorial page
appeared for the nominal editor Lawrence A. Audrain (1910–1957).
Lengthy features on both the store of wood type at The Glad Hand Press (a
nonprofit organization belonging to RCA-Victor Records art director Robert
M. Jones) and Cooper Union's calligraphy dominated the content. The cover,
by devout modernist Rudolph de Harak, implied the roots of *Print*'s fealty
to the old and advocacy of the new. The editorial note explained that this
second *Print* cover from de Harak was connected to the 7th International
Design Conference in Aspen.

Print XI:6

creativity issue

Print XI:6, May/June 1958

Saul Bass (cover designer)

I n a short introduction, *Print*'s managing editor Nanci A. Lyman wrote,
"This entire issue of *Print* is devoted to a single theme: creativity." The
issue began with an extensive 21-page feature on the cover designer, Saul
Bass, who was quoted as saying, "Creativity is indivisible." This was taken
to mean that "the creative process" cannot be "preserved by piecemeal, com-
mittee activity." What was the meaning of the foot on the cover? Well, many
things to many people.

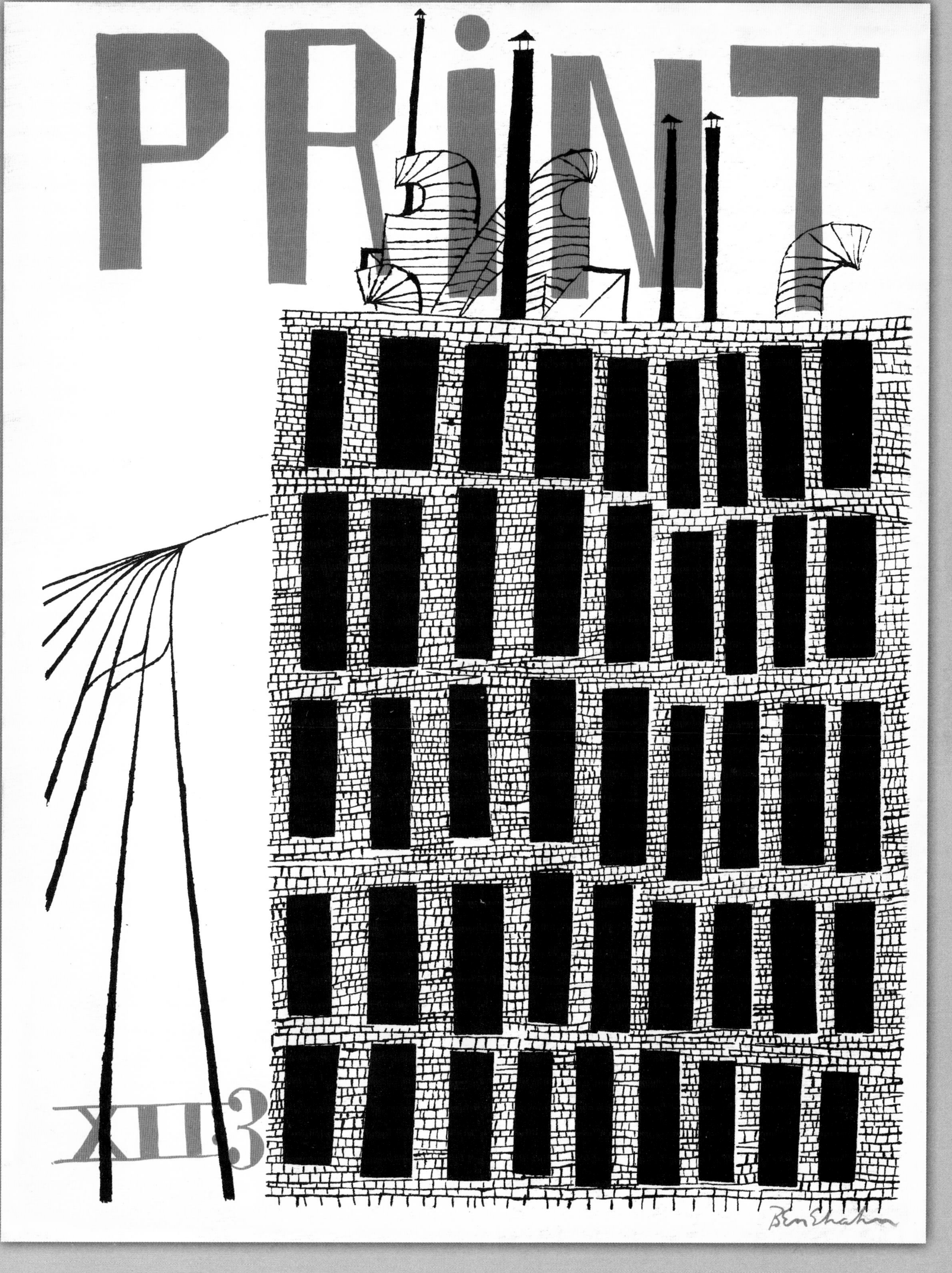
PRINT
XII 3
Ben Shahn

Print XII:3, November/December 1958

Ben Shahn (cover designer)

Phil Franznick (art director)

I n 1958, a new publisher, Milton L. Kaye, bought the magazine from the Rudge family and brought aboard a new staff to reposition *Print* as more of a trade magazine than a traditional journal on design issues and events. Ben Shahn, who was awarded Graphic Designer of the Year by *Print*, designed this cover as a tip of the hat to modernity. Thanks to the temporary removal of the Chisel type nameplate, Shahn succeeded in making his hand-drawn lettering fit neatly with his image. The editors devoted the issue to both The Graphic Designer at Work and Educating the Graphic Designer, and subjects ran the gamut from profiles of independent designers and creativity to modern art's influence on designers.

Print
XIII:3

AMERICA'S GRAPHIC DESIGN MAGAZINE
MAY-JUNE / CORPORATE IMAGE ISSUE

Print XIII:3, May/June 1959

Lou Dorfsman, Herb Lubalin (guest art directors)

B efore "branding" became both a noun *and* verb, the single most important jewel in the corporate identity crown was the logo. Art, advertising and promotion director of CBS, Lou Dorfsman, and vice president and creative director of Sudler, Hennessey & Lubalin, Herb Lubalin, guest-art directed this issue of *Print*. They were responsible for all content. The issue featured articles on IBM's "new look"; William Golden's CBS eye; the trademark as "corporate coat of arms"; and Alvin Lustig's thoughts on trademark design. The duo's gatefold cover was perhaps the most cluttered yet subtle of designs in the magazine's history.

ASPEN ISSUE

1960
Print
XIV:5 *September/October*

*America's
Graphic Design
Magazine*

Print XIV:5, September/October 1960

Herbert Pinzke (cover designer/guest art director)

When *Print* commissioned a guest art director—in this instance, the often-forgotten Herbert Pinzke—to oversee an issue, the overall format was more or less up for grabs. This issue, devoted to the 10 International Design Conferences in Aspen to date, included changes in everything from the nameplate to interior pages. Pinzke, who studied and taught at the Institute of Design in Chicago and was assistant director of the design laboratory at the Container Corporation of America, reformatted the magazine in a formidable yet subtle way. The enigmatic cover design was the most daring visual in the entire issue, alluding to the mountains of Colorado and foreshadowing the content within.

Print

AMERICA'S GRAPHIC DESIGN MAGAZINE
MARCH/APRIL 1961   PRINT XV:11

REPORT ON EUROPEAN DESIGN

Print XV:11, March/April 1961

Patrick Tilley (illustrator)

Marilyn Hoffner, Al Greenberg (co-art directors)

T his issue was noteworthy for showcasing contemporary European design. Co-art directors Marilyn Hoffner and Al Greenberg (husband-and-wife team) adapted the cover from a series of *The Sunday Times* advertisements illustrated by Patrick Tilley. Coincidentally, the issue contained a New York and Penn ad, created by Jacques Nathan-Garamond, that was part of a series of ads by various European and American designers. Ads created by Tom Eckersley, Herb Lubalin and Ladislav Sutnar appeared in previous issues, and frankly, national origins were impossible to detect based on design alone.

Print

AMERICA'S GRAPHIC DESIGN MAGAZINE
MARCH/APRIL 1962   **XVI: 2**

IN THIS ISSUE...A CURRENT LOOK AT DESIGN...DOYLE DANE BERNBACH...HIGH DESIGN
IQ FOR HIGH FASHION GQ...THE MAN WITH THE VERTICAL VIEW...UTOPIAN WORLD
OF THE PRIVATE PRESS...LESTER BEALL...THE DESIGNS THAT MATTER TO MATTER

Print XVI:2, March/April 1962

Al Greenberg (cover artist; cover art from an editorial page in *Gentlemen's Quarterly*)

Marilyn Hoffner (art director)

By now, advertising inserts on paper stocks of various color and weight were filling up "America's Graphic Design Magazine," making it difficult to separate editorial from advertisement (except that editorial was black and white). The editorial was more trade-centric than ever. Al Greenberg designed the cover using a piece that had appeared in *Gentlemen's Quarterly*, where he was art director, and which *Print* featured in an article. Noteworthy articles included one on Lester Beall's writing and design, as well as "Designs That Matter to Herbert Matter."

AMERICA'S GRAPHIC DESIGN MAGAZINE
SEPTEMBER/OCTOBER 1962
PRINT XVI:V

Print

CHERMAYEFF & GEISMAR ASSOCIATES

Print XVI:V, September/October 1962

Chermayeff & Geismar Associates (cover design)

Andrew P. Kner (art director)

In 1962, the design industry saw big changes, and *Print* did, too. This cover, designed by Chermayeff & Geismar Associates, introduced the magazine's feature about the duo only two years after their partner, Robert Brownjohn, left for England. The article made the point that Chermayeff & Geismar deliberately distinguished their practice from a design studio, instead calling it a design office. Their practice was built not on a specific style or discipline, but on diverse products, from corporate identity to "'small' items which permit a more immediate design solution." More *Print* news in 1962 included the addition of Martin Fox as executive editor (with Arnold Farber as editor) and Andrew P. Kner as art director. Gradually, the trade ethos of the magazine would become more journalistic and begin covering design culture.

AMERICA'S GRAPHIC DESIGN MAGAZINE
MAY/JUNE 1963
PRINT XVII:III

Print

Print Media: Circa 1963

Print XVII:III, May/June 1963

Andrew P. Kner (cover designer/art director)

T he theme for this issue, Print Media: Circa 1963, was a strange a
malgam with a cover that was equally as strange. It was, in fact, the
second installment of the January/February 1963 issue, which had
been devoted to "Great Print Media Success Stories." The editors noted that
their "intention was to 'beat the drums' for the print medium—a joyful noise,
richly deserved." Continuing with parts II and III, *Print* featured sections on
"Changing Trends in Five Major Print Categories," including an article on the
Container Corporation of America's veteran designer, Albert Kner (Andrew
P. Kner's father), and packaging of the future. Part III showed "Capsule Print
Media Success Stories," including a look at *Monocle* magazine, art directed by
Lou Klein and Phil Gips.

AMERICA'S GRAPHIC DESIGN MAGAZINE
JULY/AUGUST 1965
PRINT XIX:IV

Print

IN THIS ISSUE:
GRAPHIC DESIGN
FOR THE
PERFORMING ARTS

ALSO:
8TH ANNUAL
PAPER SECTION

Print XIX:IV, July/August 1965

Andrew P. Kner (cover designer/art director)

Many of *Print*'s issues were offering readers detailed reports and careful analysis on a variety of themes, including the hot ticket of Graphic Design for the Performing Arts. This included film posters, film titles, TV graphics, TV promotion and graphics for live performances. The market for graphics in these genres was growing, and *Print* rightly saw an opening for coverage. Andrew P. Kner took on the challenge of designing graphics to represent all of these, and he accomplished this simply and without fanfare. *Print*'s subtle covers were often its best.

AMERICA'S GRAPHIC DESIGN MAGAZINE
SEPTEMBER/OCTOBER 1965
PRINT XIX:V

Print

Print XIX:V, September/October 1965

Arlene La Rotonda (cover designer)

Andrew P. Kner (art director)

It is perplexing that some of *Print*'s finest covers, such as this one by Arlene La Rotonda, were created by students for the magazine's Annual Cover Design Competition. Yet the design community never again heard from many of these student designers, at least not through the design magazines or annuals. This cover was among a few, past and present, to reference the tattoo as a subset of graphic design and illustration. Also in this issue, a feature on visual journalist Feliks Topolski revealed his self-published *Topolski's Chronicles* for the first time in an American context.

AMERICA'S GRAPHIC DESIGN MAGAZINE
JULY/AUGUST 1966
PRINT XX:IV

Print

Print XX:IV, July/August 1966

Andrew P. Kner (cover designer/art director)

This cover served as a subtly profound visual commentary—a sampling of the world's red, white and blue national flags, including the U.S. and North Korea. The issue's lead story on the subject of the graphics of dissent asked the question, "Who says public affairs magazines have to be visually dull?" Another story, "Graphic Uplift in Downtown Chicago," provided some balance, exploring how civic banners and posters played a part in the city's revitalization. These are just two examples of how *Print* foresaw the role of graphic design in socio-political discourse and brought it smartly into the emerging design discourse.

AMERICA'S GRAPHIC DESIGN MAGAZINE
SEPTEMBER/OCTOBER 1966
PRINT XX:V

Print **XX:V, September/October 1966**

David Caplan (cover designer)

Andrew P. Kner (art director)

Another student, another cover. This time, a conceptually enigmatic, yet graphically striking image by David Caplan won the 3rd Annual Cover Design Competition. Coincidentally, it covered an issue that featured a story about trends in campus graphics. "The communications needs of colleges and universities are very [much] like those of corporations," wrote Michael A. Schacht. To round off the educational package, *Print* showcased three undergrad design projects that were "fresh, fervent, provoking." The magazine was also compelled to offer its analysis of design from Eastern Europe by giving up "clues to [the] present state of Cold War tensions."

AMERICA'S GRAPHIC DESIGN MAGAZINE
NOVEMBER/DECEMBER 1966
SPECIAL REPRINT EDITION

THE DESIGNER AND THE COMPUTER

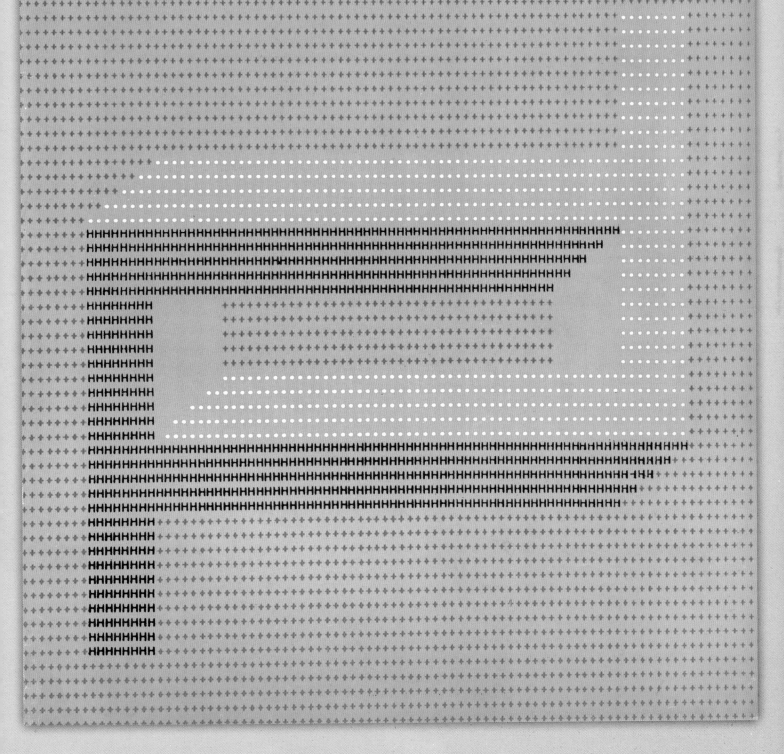

Print XX:VI, November/December 1966

Martin Krampen (cover designer)

Veljo Taht (programmer)

Andrew P. Kner (art director)

IBM 7040/1401 (execution)

---

*P*rint's portfolio included coverage of the computer age decades prior to the digital revolution. This issue focused on the primitive period of graphic design in the technological world, so the editors made sure to make a semantic clarification: "The authors of the articles herein, which deal with various aspects of design and computers, for the most part use the words 'graphics' and 'design' in the broad sense to mean two-dimensional visualizations of ideas (sometimes extremely complex and abstract ideas). In only a few cases are these terms used to connote the kind of creative problem-solving involved in producing communications of various types—the sense in which 'graphic design' is normally used in these pages."

AMERICA'S GRAPHIC DESIGN MAGAZINE
SEPTEMBER/OCTOBER 1967
PRINT XXI:V

Print

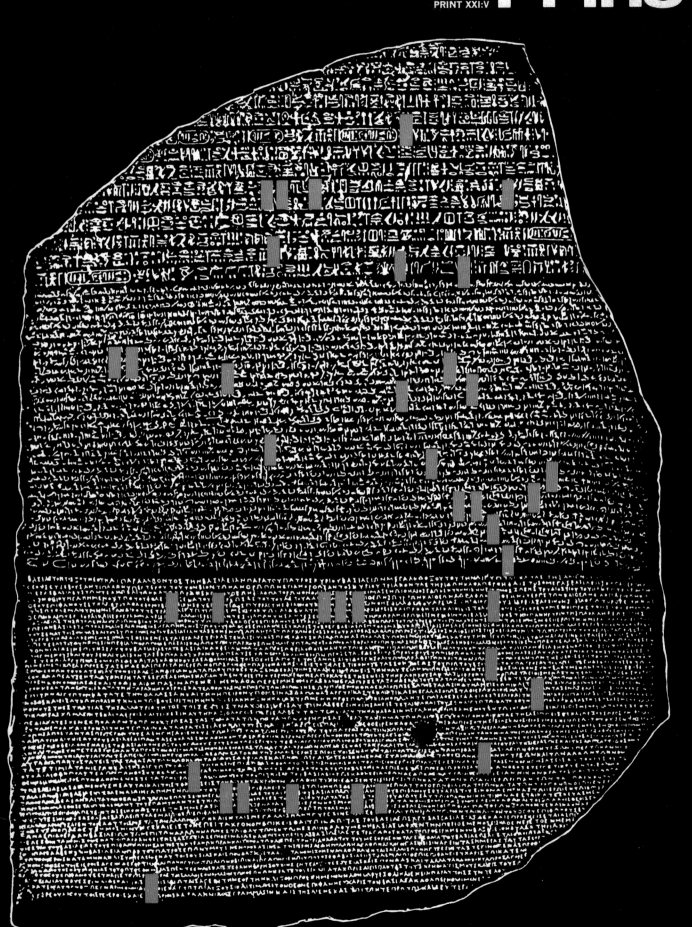

Print XXI:V, September/October 1967

Richard Scott (cover designer)

Andrew P. Kner (art director)

---

*P*rint's Annual Cover Design Competition opened to only students in 1967. Richard Scott of Richmond Professional Institute in Virginia designed the winning entry featured here. "His pithy summation of the history of communication was well conceived and executed," wrote vice president and editor Martin Fox. "It works as a cover—which many of the [other] entries failed to do." Critical remarks like this were part of the magazine's editorial voice.

AMERICA'S GRAPHIC DESIGN MAGAZINE
SEPTEMBER/OCTOBER 1968
PRINT XXII:V

Print

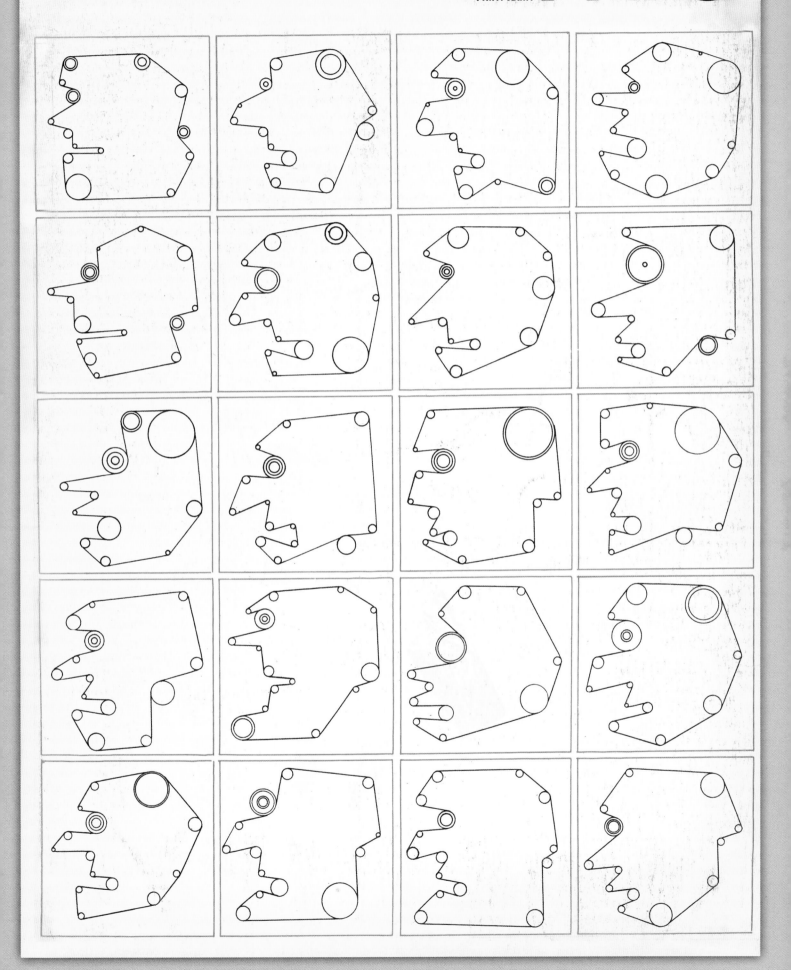

Print XXII:V, September/October 1968

Hartmut Jäger (cover designer)
Andrew P. Kner (art director)

If there is an abundance of Annual Cover Design Competition (note that the title was always changing) covers in this book, it is because they were often off the beaten track. This year the competition became an international event, including entries from several European art and design schools. "The infusion of cover ideas from abroad is perhaps one reason why the overall level of entries was fairly high," wrote Martin Fox. The jury included *Look* art director William Hopkins, illustrator Paul Davis and Mead Library of Ideas director Joseph A. Messina, as well as Andrew P. Kner, Tom Geismar and Herb Lubalin. Despite Fox's observation that "at least most of the judges this year were happier with the entries than previous years' judges have been," the judges were not greatly impressed. Geismar said, "In my view, about 10 percent of the entries were very good; perhaps that isn't a bad average." Lubalin said, "I would say that the quality of this year's covers is generally poor. ... I would make a general recommendation that communications students spend less time at the drawing board and more time observing what's happening, baby!" Hartmut Jäger's cover was nonetheless distinctive.

AMERICA'S GRAPHIC DESIGN MAGAZINE
NOVEMBER/DECEMBER 1968
PRINT XXII:VI

Print

Barbara Nessim

Print XXII:VI, November/December 1968

Barbara Nessim (cover illustrator)

Andrew P. Kner (art director)

New York artist Barbara Nessim was one of the first significant women illustrators working in a primarily male-dominated profession. She had a lyrical style that was suggestive and symbolic and built a reputation for transcending the clichés of a field built on realism. Frequent editorial work helped solidify her place in illustration history. "There are virtually no differences either in style or point of view between the work which Miss Nessim does for herself and that which she does for commercial clients," wrote associate art director Carol Stevens in the cover story. That lack of duality between art and commercial art was highly valued by *Print*'s editors.

THIRTIETH ANNIVERSARY YEAR

AMERICA'S GRAPHIC DESIGN MAGAZINE
NOVEMBER/DECEMBER 1969
PRINT XXIII:VI

Print

International Signs and Symbols:

Special ICOGRADA Issue

Print XXIII:VI, November/December 1969

Jean-Michel Folon (cover artist)

Andrew P. Kner (art director)

Belgian-born Jean-Michel Folon (*nom de crayon* Folon; 1934–2005) was an ingenious illustrator and cartoonist, prolific in both advertising and editorial. His approach stood out for his conceptual intelligence, comic surrealism and inventive glyphs and arrows that poked fun at conformist society. *Print*'s art director, Andrew P. Kner, wisely assigned Folon to illustrate the theme of International Signs and Symbols. Folon's image cautioned the viewer not to rely on authority of any kind, considering that in general, international signs and symbols are designed to inform and direct behavior but often dictate and confuse.

AMERICA'S GRAPHIC DESIGN MAGAZINE
MAY/JUNE 1970
PRINT XXIV: III

Print

Print XXIV:III, May/June 1970

Andrew P. Kner (cover designer/art director)

P*rint*'s political coverage often generated protest letters from readers who strongly objected to what they perceived as New York liberal partisanship sullying their design coverage. By 1970, feminism was a long-overdue fact of American life, but it was still a controversial subject. Andrew P. Kner's cover, a witty sample of the ultra-romantic "Liberty Leading the People" by Eugène Delacroix, represented the story "Women's Lib and Women Designers." The piece noted that, even then, women's salaries were lower than men's. Surprise?

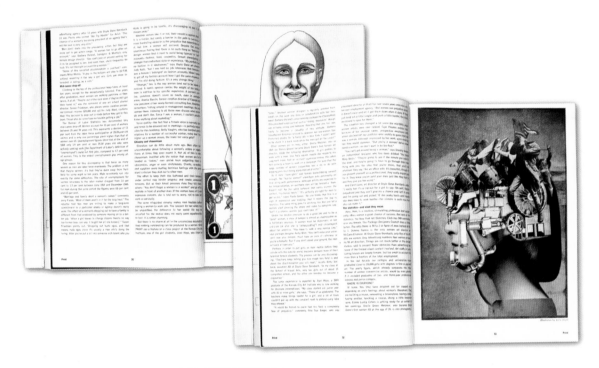

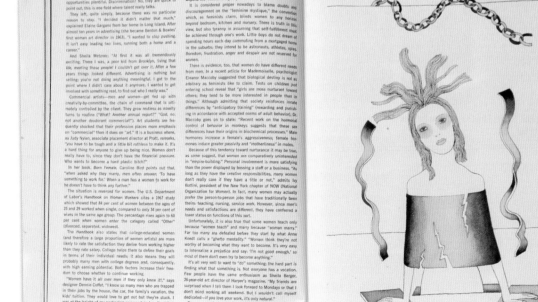

AMERICA'S GRAPHIC DESIGN MAGAZINE
SEPTEMBER/OCTOBER 1971
PRINT XXV:V

Print

Print XXV:V, September/October 1971

Jerry Loren Kuyper (cover designer)

Andrew P. Kner (art director)

Yet another winner of *Print*'s Annual Cover Design Competition, this stark landscape of cubicles by Jerry Loren Kuyper from the University of Cincinnati may have seemed depressing if one were looking for a job in a competitive environment, but it was, and still is, nonetheless a heartfelt representation of the average student before graduation. "After a couple of years in which the caliber of entries … noticeably declined, it is pleasant to report that the entries for the 1971 competition showed a distinct improvement," wrote Martin Fox with characteristic frankness. True enough, but alas Fox's stronger statements were less optimistic.

AMERICA'S GRAPHIC DESIGN MAGAZINE
SEPTEMBER/OCTOBER 1972
PRINT XXVI:V

Print

Print XXVI:V, September/October 1972

Linda Brooks Stillman (cover designer)

Andrew P. Kner (art director)

The role of most *Print* covers has always been to visually define the essence of graphic design and visual communications. Linda Brooks Stillman's image was another of *Print*'s graffiti references, suggesting that the past is inextricably linked to the present. Stillman's complex yet simple cover compared cultural antiquity and contemporary detritus as all of a piece. The issue featured a haunting photo essay by Mark Haven, Miho's personal response to the folk art of Brazil, and Jan Faust's biting view of American life.

AMERICA'S GRAPHIC DESIGN MAGAZINE
SEPTEMBER/OCTOBER 1974
PRINT XXVIII:V

Print

Print XXVIII:V, September/October 1974

István Orosz (cover designer)

Andrew P. Kner (art director)

I stván Orosz (born 1951) is one of Hungary's most prolific poster artists. He was just beginning his illustrious career when he conceived his popular, transformational—and what Orosz calls an "anamorphoses"— alphabet as a cover. This was an early example of a trend in metamorphic and otherwise naturally found lettering that has erupted in the digital age.

AMERICA'S GRAPHIC DESIGN MAGAZINE
JULY/AUGUST 1975
PRINT XXIX:IV

Print

Le-Tan

Print XXIX:IV, July/August 1975

Pierre Le-Tan (cover illustrator)

Andrew P. Kner (art director)

French native Pierre Le-Tan (born 1950) was up-and-coming in the illustration world in 1975. His work was beginning to make its mark on *The New Yorker* covers and in *The New York Times*. Known for his intricate yet unconventional cross-hatching, he took a comically deadpan approach to his subjects and also enjoyed replicating the treasures of the bourgeoisie. His characteristic wry wit and elegant drawing style were unmistakable on this cover.

AMERICA'S GRAPHIC DESIGN MAGAZINE
JANUARY/FEBRUARY 1976
PRINT XXX:I

Print

STAN MACK'S REAL LIFE FUNNIES

The Design Scene

GUARANTEE: ALL DIALOGUE IS RECORDED VERBATIM

Print XXX:I, January/February 1976

Stan Mack (cover illustrator)

Andrew P. Kner (art director)

Stan Mack's "Real Life Funnies" originally appeared in New York City's *The Village Voice*. Long before reality TV captured audiences' hearts and minds—and made fools of many participants—Mack reported real-life monologues and dialogues that he overheard in a variety of social and professional venues. For *Print*, he covered the design scene, and although the characters may not have looked exactly like the real folks, their words were taken verbatim, exactly as they were spoken. As they say, nothing's stranger than truth.

AMERICA'S GRAPHIC DESIGN MAGAZINE
MARCH/APRIL 1977
PRINT XXXI:II

Print

Print XXXI:II, March/April 1977

Rick Meyerowitz (cover designer)

Andrew P. Kner (art director)

Rick Meyerowitz (born 1943) was best known for his *National Lampoon* cover of "Mona Gorilla," a parody of the famous Mona Lisa. His cover comically showed the dangers of the freelance life. Inside, his caricatures were showcased in "Utter Madness" by Valerie F. Brooks, who wrote that Meyerowitz's "delight at being a cartoonist is equaled only by his amazement at his own abilities … and output."

AMERICA'S GRAPHIC DESIGN MAGAZINE
NOVEMBER/DECEMBER 1978
PRINT XXXII:VI

Print

Print XXXII:VI, November/December 1978

Jack Lefkowitz (cover designer)

Andrew P. Kner (art director)

I n 1978, Brooklyn-born Jack Lefkowitz was a bit of a sensation. His work was startling for the least likely magazine imaginable for award-winning design: the *Industrial Launderer*, the organ of the Institute for Industrial Launderers in Washington, DC. By the time *Print* featured Lefkowitz, he had been working for the Institute for 11 years. In addition to all its printed materials, Lefkowitz's team designed the flagship journal using his illustrations for each of its covers, in the style of this *Print* issue.

Robert Weaver's
Illustration Issue

FORTIETH ANNIVERSARY YEAR

AMERICA'S GRAPHIC DESIGN MAGAZINE
NOVEMBER/DECEMBER 1979
PRINT XXXIII:VI

Print

Print XXXIII:VI, November/December 1979

Robert Weaver (cover illustrator)

Andrew P. Kner (art director)

R arely did *Print* give an issue to a single guest editor, but an exception was made for American illustrator Robert Weaver (1924–1994), who was considered the preeminent expressionist illustrator of his time. His work, an amalgam of abstract and representational sensibilities, influenced a generation of post-Rockwellian conceptualists. He was a popular teacher, who in his later years tragically lost eyesight. *Print* conceived this issue as Weaver neared total blindness. It featured Weaver's "casual and highly informal sampling" of contemporaries and younger illustrators; works by Barbara Nessim, Milton Glaser, Seymour Chwast and Anita Siegel made the cut. An interview with Weaver, conducted by Weaver, stated: "I am painfully aware that many people are not present. How [could I] ignore the likes of Steinberg, for example? Or Paul Davis? Or Ed Sorel, and others? But then, I haven't included myself, either."

Print XXXV:III, May/June 1981

Art Spiegelman (cover illustrator)

Andrew P. Kner (art director)

With the publication in 1980 of *Maus: A Survivor's Tale*, Art Spiegelman, among others, forever changed the public's perception of comics and helped to launch the "graphic novel" revolution. This cover represented Spiegelman's view of the comic strip as a brilliant invention with endless expressive possibilities. It was also the frontispiece of a feature story about *RAW*, the experimental comics magazine edited by Spiegelman and Francois Mouly. *RAW* had originally serialized *Maus,* and it arguably introduced the world to an entirely new concept in pictorial narrative. The comics magazine further signaled a shift in sex-and-drug "underground comix" to more mature introspective and autobiographical comix.

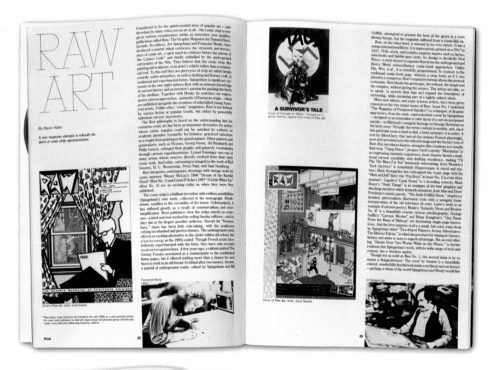

$5

Print

AMERICA'S GRAPHIC DESIGN MAGAZINE
MAY/JUNE 1982
PRINT XXXVI:III

Sempé.

Print XXXVI:III, May/June 1982

Jean-Jacques Sempé (cover artist)

Andrew P. Kner (art director)

French cartoonist Jean-Jacques Sempé (born 1932), known as Sempé, enjoyed a large American audience, partly owing to his frequent work in *The New Yorker* magazine. He was the featured artist in this issue, with the piece focusing on his rather gentle but acerbic depictions of the *Comédie humaine*, which were decidedly French in idiom but universal in conception. His interest in social contradiction was evident in this cover.

$5
Print
AMERICA'S GRAPHIC DESIGN MAGAZINE
MAY/JUNE 1984
PRINT XXXVIII:III

Print XXXVIII:III, May/June 1984

Matt Mahurin (cover artist)

Andrew P. Kner (art director)

---

*P*rint deemed Matt Mahurin ready for prime-time coverage at only 25. In fact, almost immediately after the California native graduated from Art Center, he received a major commission from *Time* magazine to illustrate a cover story on the subject of "private violence." The *Time* article and art received unprecedented attention, which put Mahurin on the map. He consistently integrated photography and painting, so it was not surprising that years after this feature in *Print* he became a photographer and film director. His cover for this issue, using his early signature method, symbolically addressed the balance between art and commerce, a recurring *Print* theme. This issue also took a look at alternative visual cultures, something *Print* covered frequently. "Joking with Death" introduced how Mexican artisans used skulls and skeletons as social and political satire.

$5

Print

AMERICA'S GRAPHIC DESIGN MAGAZINE
JANUARY/FEBRUARY 1985
PRINT XXXIX:I

Print XXXIX:I, January/February 1985

Cipe Pineles (cover artist)

Andrew P. Kner (art director)

Austrian-born Cipe Pineles (1908–1991) immigrated to New York when she was 14 years old. She later became one of America's leading art directors—indeed one of the foremost women in a male-dominated field. Initially an assistant at Condé Nast to legendary Dr. M.F. Agha, she eventually took the helm of *Glamour* and *Seventeen*, where she had the freedom to work with progressive illustration and high-end photography. As a painter, she understood composition and could empathize with contributors. Her last hurrah was as a teacher at Otis-Parsons as well as designer of its promotional materials. This *Print* cover—and the accompanying extensive feature article by Carol Stevens—was Pineles' last substantial magazine coverage prior to a monograph on her life's work by Martha Scotford.

SPECIAL GRAPHIC PARODY SECTION

$7.50

AMERICA'S GRAPHIC DESIGN MAGAZINE
NOVEMBER/DECEMBER 1985
PRINT XXXIX:VI

Print

THE COMPLETE GENEALOGY OF GRAPHIC DESIGN

KEY — **m** — MARRIED — **c** — CHILD OF — **d** — DESCENDED FROM — ILLICIT LIAISON

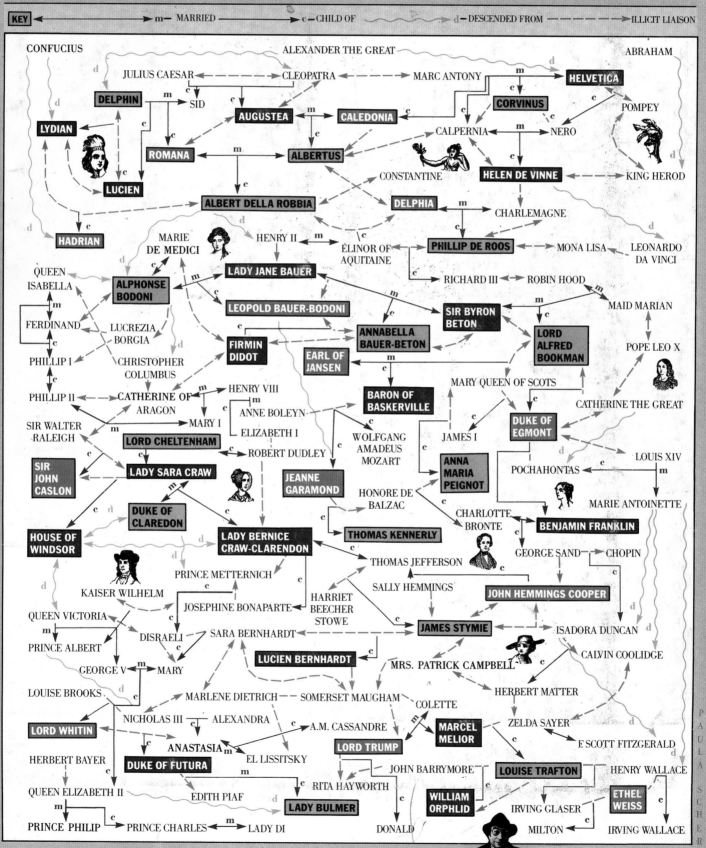

PAULA SCHER

Print XXXIX:VI, November/December 1985

Paula Scher, Koppel & Scher (cover art)

---

66 It's been 11 years since *Print* last published a special graphic parody section, and not having much else to do, we figure we might as well do another one," said *Print*'s editors, who went on to note that Paula Scher and Steven Heller "did the entire section, so don't yell at us." Included were stories on the master of Swiss design, AnaleRetentiv, the influence of Walter Keane on American illustration, and the corporate identity of Canada. But it was Scher's "The Complete Genealogy of Graphic Design" cover that spoke reams of hilarious gibberish about the timeline of interrelationships, cross-breeding and bastard children that became modern graphic design.

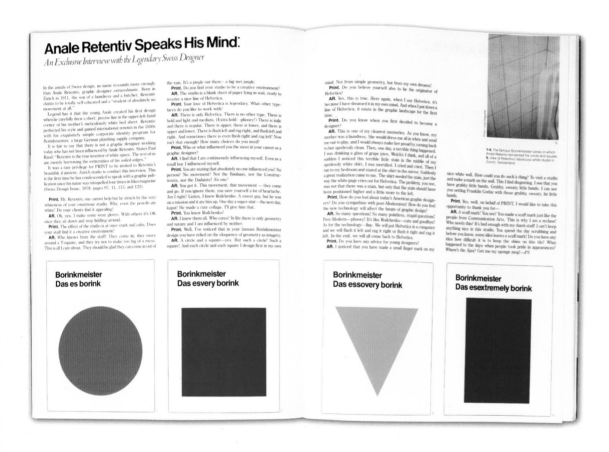

$25

Print

AMERICA'S GRAPHIC DESIGN MAGAZINE
JULY/AUGUST 1986
PRINT XL:IV

Print's Regional Design Annual 1986

Print XL:IV, July/August 1986

Bill Nelson (cover artist)

Andrew P. Kner (art director)

It was a challenge year after year to devise a new cover for *Print*'s Regional Design Annual. This year's was among the best of the best. Illustrated by precisionist and figurative artist Bill Nelson, the stamp motif was a spot-on convincing *trompe l'oeil*. Subsequent covers were not always as conceptually acute, but this was admittedly a hard act to follow.

$6

AMERICA'S GRAPHIC DESIGN MAGAZINE
JANUARY/FEBRUARY 1987
PRINT XLI:I

Print

Print XLI:I, January/February 1987

Philippe Weisbecker (cover artist)

Andrew P. Kner (art director)

Paris native Philippe Weisbecker (born 1942) came to prominence as an illustrator for *The New York Times* Op-Ed page during the early 1970s. His surrealist cross-hatched drawings fit the so-called *Times'* Op-Ed style, which was influenced by Roland Topor. Weisbecker was interested in breaking this bond and would frequently try various other approaches and styles. This *Print* cover represented one of those creative transformations that he found could function in the post–Op-Ed illustration environment. He subsequently went further into abstraction and primitivism.

$6
AMERICA'S GRAPHIC DESIGN MAGAZINE
MAY/JUNE 1987
PRINT XLI:III

Print

Print XLI:III, May/June 1987

Gottfried Helnwein (cover artist)

Andrew P. Kner (art director)

Austrian-born Gottfried Helnwein, a hyperrealist painter with a penchant for grotesque and terrifying imagery involving children in danger, was popular in magazines like *Time* and *Rolling Stone*. His meticulously detailed depictions of violence were somehow mitigated by the enviable craft that he brought to each piece. This cover, related to a feature on his work to date, was one of the few intensely emotional works deemed suitable for *Print*. At the same time, however, it was one of Helnwein's signature disturbing views of childhood emotions.

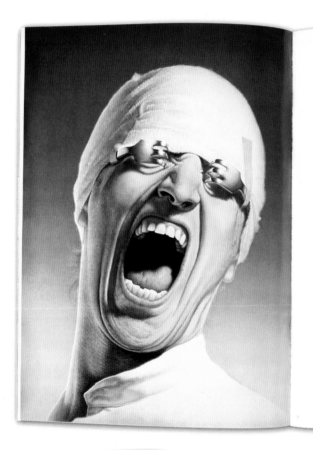

$6

Print

AMERICA'S GRAPHIC DESIGN MAGAZINE
JANUARY/FEBRUARY 1988
PRINT XLII:1

Print XLII:I, January/February 1988

Edward Gorey (cover artist)

Andrew P. Kner (art director)

Visual storyteller Edward Gorey (1925–2000) was a favorite among the editors at *Print*. So when the time finally came to feature his work, it was imperative to have an original cover by him as well. The Print or Perish theme was perfect for the magazine that promoted print in all its forms, and Gorey's signature black-and-white, cross-hatched characters were a must. He added color in the serpents (symbolizing the editors, perhaps) and the dog's mustache (of course). Don't forget to look at the blimp.

$6

AMERICA'S GRAPHIC DESIGN MAGAZINE
MAY/JUNE 1988
PRINT XLII:III

Print

Print XLII:III, May/June 1988

James McMullan (cover designer)

Jerry Orabona (cover photography)

Andrew P. Kner (art director)

James McMullan (born 1934) and his theater posters were box-office hits. Well, at least around New York City the visual gems certainly enlivened the streets and enhanced the theater poster genre, which was not as glorious as it had once been. The imperative to include headliners' names challenged designers to create good pieces. Along with the work of Paul Davis, McMullan's work made a difference. So, rather than commission an exclusive *Print* cover to accompany a feature on McMullan, Andrew P. Kner selected a photograph of a bus poster that had become a fixture of the city.

$7.50

AMERICA'S GRAPHIC DESIGN MAGAZINE
SEPTEMBER/OCTOBER 1991
PRINT XLV:V

Print

Print XLV:V, September/October 1991

Howard Ian Schiller (cover designer)

Leslie Sawin (cover illustrator)

Andrew P. Kner (art director)

In March 1985, *Print* published its first story about René Magritte as an advertising illustrator. Georges Roque wrote, "The great surrealist hated making ads—he did so only to survive. Ironically, he is a potent source of inspiration for contemporary advertising." As such, Magritte's work was frequently used as the basis of parody and satire by contemporary illustrators. This cover, which sampled Magritte's "The Treachery of Images" and coincided with the nascent part of the computer-design revolution, made the point that readers of the magazine were the drivers of computers, not the driven.

$7.50

AMERICA'S GRAPHIC DESIGN MAGAZINE
MARCH/APRIL 1992
PRINT XLVI:II

Print

Print XLVI:II, March/April 1992

John Hersey (cover artist)

Andrew P. Kner (art director)

By 1992, the computer was no longer a novelty but an increasingly essential tool in the life and work of illustrators and designers. John Hersey (born 1954) was an early adopter of digital technology as part of an oeuvre that included computer-aided and handmade imagery. His work on the cover of *Print* marked a break with the past and signaled that *Print* would soon be devoting more space to screen-based work.

$7.50

AMERICA'S GRAPHIC DESIGN MAGAZINE
SEPTEMBER/OCTOBER 1992
PRINT XLVI:V

Print

Print XLVI:V, September/October 1992

Gábor Domján (cover designer)

Andrew P. Kner (art director)

The number of times that Edvard Munch's "The Scream" has been quoted, sampled or parodied is anybody's guess. As in the case of René Magritte's work, playing around with Munch is one of the quintessential student tropes. But Gábor Domján's cover transcends the common "Home Alone" approach with the introduction of the terrified doll. As managing editor Julie Lasky wrote about the 29th International Student Cover Design Competition first-prize selection, "Many of this year's entries featured in-your-face imagery designed to shock."

$7.50

AMERICA'S GRAPHIC DESIGN MAGAZINE
JANUARY/FEBRUARY 1993
PRINT XLVII:I

Print

Print XLVII:I, January/February 1993

Edward Sorel (cover artist)

Andrew P. Kner (art director)

Caricaturist Edward Sorel (born 1929) is arguably among the most devoted enemies of political and social folly. As the title ("A Political Animal") of the profile in this issue implied, he hunted a certain kind of wily game. His cover was not only hilariously self-effacing, but it was Sorel's job description: to strip his prey bare and find their weakest physical links. Here, he slyly depicted his worst nightmare. Gut-wrenchingly funny.

$10

AMERICA'S GRAPHIC DESIGN MAGAZINE
NOVEMBER/DECEMBER 1993
PRINT XLVII:VI

Print

THE
ITALIAN
ISSUE

Print XLVII:VI, November/December 1993

Milton Glaser (cover artist)

Andrew P. Kner (art director)

I taly, in addition to France and England, is the birthplace of Western typefaces and the home of great traditions in corporate, book and magazine design. Milton Glaser (born 1929) illustrated the cover of this special Italian issue guest-edited by Museum of Modern Art curator Paola Antonelli. As a devoted Italophile, Glaser's drawing and painting styles have been molded by Italian art. Here, he elegantly employed the iconic cypress trees that rise from the rich Italian soil, transformed to symbolize the nation, the flag and both its classical and modern art.

$7.50

AMERICA'S GRAPHIC DESIGN MAGAZINE
JANUARY/FEBRUARY 1995
PRINT XLIX:I

Print

Print XLIX:I, January/February 1995

Henrik Drescher (cover illustrator)

Andrew P. Kner (art director)

*P*rint has featured its share of collage, which was an extremely popular commercial art form during the 1970s and 1980s. Danish-born Henrik Drescher (born 1955) built a visual language out of found photos, stamps and engravings, on and over which he painted and drew absurdist imagery. As a children's book illustrator, he began more or less traditionally but experimented with collage to see how far he could push the medium on his audience. This cover was typical of his fondness for visual chaos.

$7.50

AMERICA'S GRAPHIC DESIGN MAGAZINE
MAY/JUNE 1995
PRINT XLIX:III

Print

THE ELEPHANT

VANISHE

JAZZ

James Ellroy

—Haruki Murakami

Print XLIX:III, May/June 1995

Chip Kidd (cover designer)

Andrew P. Kner (art director)

By 1995, the digital revolution was in full swing, and stylistically it was evolving into an era of typographic and pictorial layering. This issue of *Print* featured a story ("Run with the Dwarves and Win") devoted to the book jackets and covers of New York–based designer Chip Kidd (born 1964). For the issue's cover, Kidd created what looked like a printer's make-ready proof showing elements of some of his cover designs. For the casual viewer, chaos reigned, but for the close reader, it all made sense.

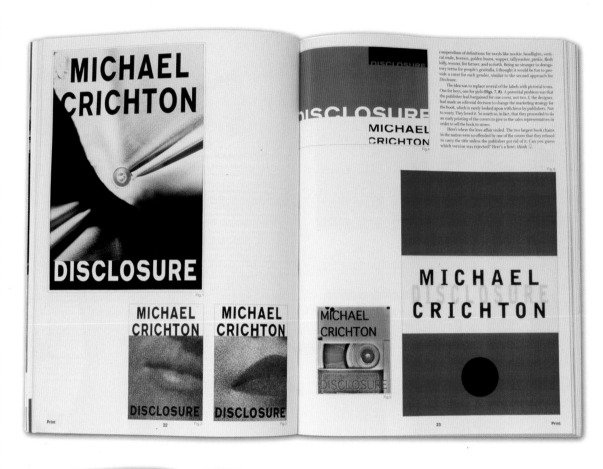

$7.50

AMERICA'S GRAPHIC DESIGN MAGAZINE
MAY/JUNE 1996
PRINT L: III

Print

Print L:III, May/June 1996

Paula Scher/Pentagram (cover design)

Andrew P. Kner (art director)

To announce *Print*'s new size and format, Paula Scher's (born 1948) concept was as WYSIWYG—what you see is what you get—as it gets by showing the trim size of the cover as the image on the cover. She employed a typographic language similar to the bold carnivalesque, show-card approach that distinguished her work for the New York Public Theater, which was showcased in a feature story. With this first redesign in more than 20 years, *Print* was poised in 1996 to enter the 21st century.

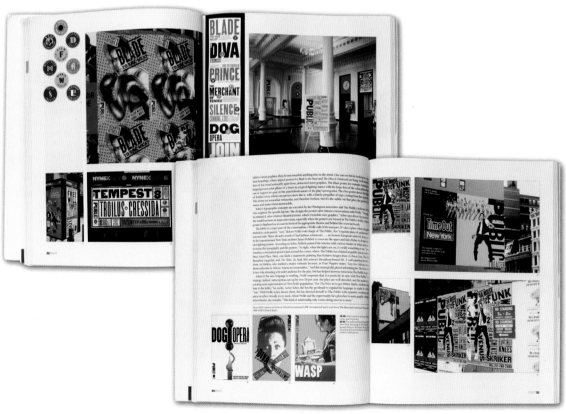

Print

$19.50

AMERICA'S GRAPHIC DESIGN MAGAZINE
JULY/AUGUST 1997
PRINT LI:IV

INCLUDING DIGITAL ART & DESIGN ANNUAL 5

Print LI:IV, July/August 1997

R.O. Blechman (cover illustrator)

Andrew P. Kner (art director)

---

*P*rint revered the pioneers in the field, and R.O. Blechman (born 1930) is arguably a form-giver in the realm of minimalist cartooning. Blechman was featured in a piece about *Story* magazine, a journal of contemporary fiction, for which he produced a series of covers that invited experimentation. For this *Print* cover, he employed his signature simplicity to show the personality difference between a quiet period and a boisterous exclamation point. The only flaw in this otherwise perfect concept was the blue bar at the bottom announcing the Digital Art and Design Annual. How beautiful the cover would've been in only black, white and red.

Print LI:V, September/October 1997

Chris Ware (cover designer)

Andrew P. Kner (art director)

Coming on the heels of Blechman's cover, this next issue of the year was diametrically the opposite of simplicity, although the quintessence of precision. Chris Ware (born 1967)—known for his "Acme Novelty Library" comic strips that refer to 19th-century comic book, advertising and magazine conventions—produced a cover for *Print*'s Regional Design Annual that was both vintage and fresh. He drew and lettered everything by hand, including the standard *Print* logo.

Print

AMERICA'S GRAPHIC DESIGN MAGAZINE

PRINT LIII:I

including
new visual
artists
review!

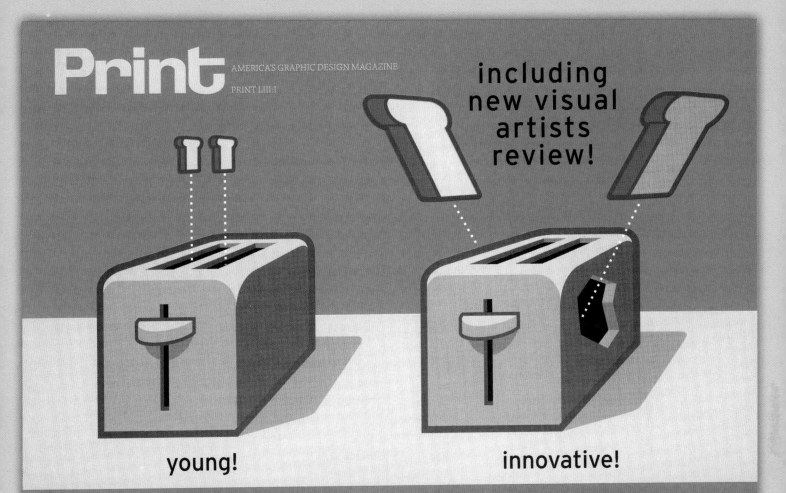

young!

innovative!

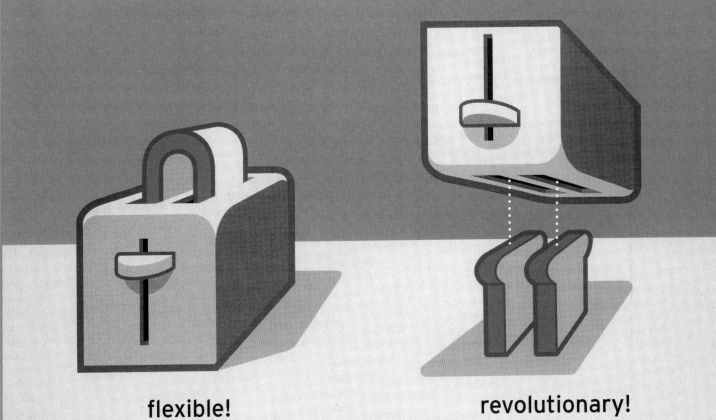

flexible!

revolutionary!

Print LIII:I, January/February 1999

Christoph Niemann (cover designer)

Andrew P. Kner (art director)

German-born Christoph Niemann (born 1970) represented the post-Blechman generation of graphic humorists. His irony and metaphoric wit found outlet in many of the leading magazines. To illustrate the New Visual Artists Review, he used the toaster as a clever metaphor for what was hot and getting hotter. Niemann's schematic-infographic-deadpan style enhanced his young, innovative, flexible and revolutionary sense of comedy.

Print

$8

AMERICA'S GRAPHIC DESIGN MAGAZINE
MAY/JUNE 1999
PRINT LIII:III

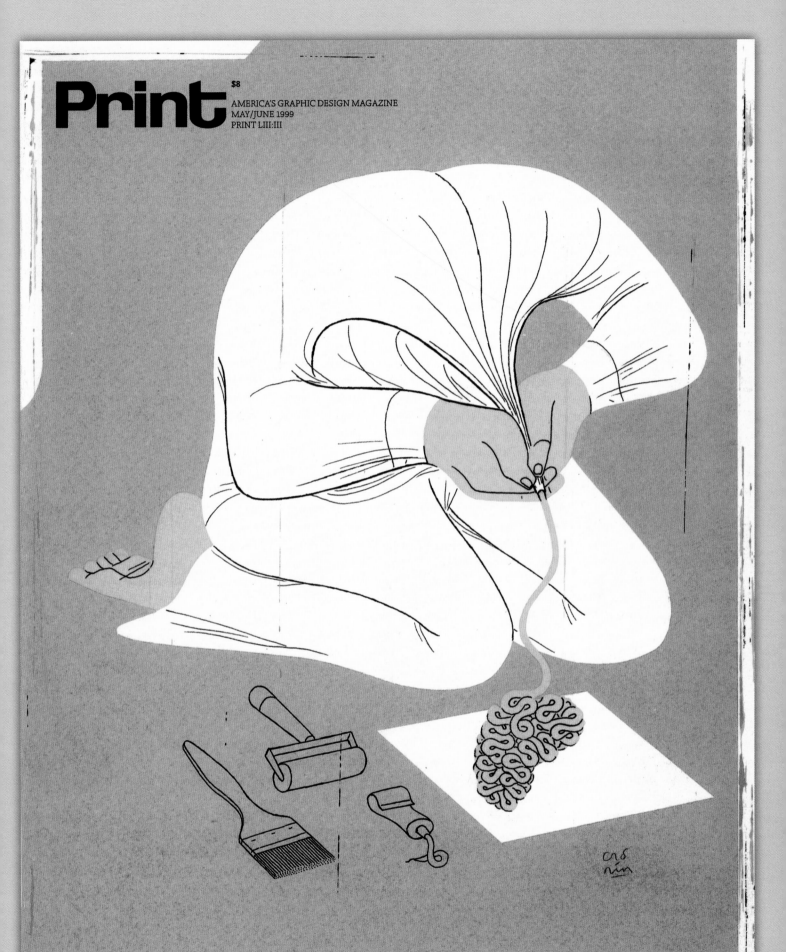

Print LIII:III, May/June 1999

Brian Cronin (cover illustrator)

Andrew P. Kner (art director)

It is difficult to imagine an image like Brian Cronin's running on a *Print* cover prior to the 1990s. Although surreal representation was commonly practiced, the bar of conceptual acerbity was raised to reflect an increase in expressive art and design. Cronin's concept was, however, typical of the extreme illustrative irony that enlightened and entertained in those fin de siècle years before the millennium.

print

America's Graphic Design Magazine

Henna Mania
Guerrilla Graphics
Calendar Girls
Phantom Books
Tibor's Teachings
Designer Filmmakers

$8 May/June 2000 Print LIV:III

Print LIV:III, May/June 2000

Barnaby Hall (cover photography)
Makiko Yoshimura (henna designer)
Steven Brower (art director)

This third issue of the new millennium marked some major baton changes at *Print*. Andrew P. Kner stepped down as the magazine's veteran art director, and Steven Brower assumed the role. Brower changed the long-standing logo for a type style and setting that was more compatible with the 9-by-10.875-inch format. The cover, which had more or less eschewed coverlines before, now had them tattooed onto flesh, illustrating the lead story "Henna Mania."

print

America's Graphic Design Magazine

NEW ECONOMY, OLD TECH
TARGETING TOBACCO
GRAFFITI BLACKBOOKS

HISTORY EX POST FACTO
SUMPTUOUS COMICS
AFRICAN ALPHABETS

$8 Print LV:III

Print LV:III, May/June 2001

Gérard DuBois (cover illustrator)

Steven Brower (art director)

Retaining *Print*'s illustrative cover tradition, Steven Brower commissioned a haunting image that was rooted in early 20th-century surrealism with a distinct contemporary attitude. Building upon a vocabulary of the 1930s through 1950s, Montreal-based Gérard DuBois skillfully injected current references that implied the solitude and sanctity of the creative process. The young painter in the picture is spreading his pigment over pieces of a *Print* logo because he's making his cover within a cover.

print

America's Graphic Design Magazine

Print's Regional Design Annual 2001

$35 Print LV:V

Print LV:V, September/October 2001

Steven Brower (cover artist/art director)

As Americans were reeling from the 9/11 attacks, *Print*'s Regional Design Annual was ready to go to press. "There was a very different cover that was due to the printer on 9/11/01," Steven Brower recalled. The *Print* offices were at the time located near the 25th St. armory, which became headquarters for the missing. "There were flyers pasted everywhere of loved ones, many featuring hearts," Brower said. There was no way he could send out the original cover in the light of those events. "I knew I wanted to echo the sentiments of those who had lost loved ones, and I knew of no other heart better than Milton's to represent New York," he continued. "I created the crack originating lower left in the area where we were attacked and sent it off the printer." The original art—featuring an antique bank and a clown holding a hoop through which a dog jumped, depositing the coin in the slot—was printed in the table of contents.

Print LVI:I, March/April 2002

Ewa Zerger (cover artist)

Steven Brower (art director)

The winner of *Print*'s 38th Annual Student Cover Design Competition was first among 173 entries and "fulfilled the requirement of a good idea well-executed," wrote Robert Treadway. Ewe Zerger said, "I looked at what a magazine is. … It's a soapbox, a forum for writers and readers—in this case, designers—to say what they want to say." She added, "The spin came about because you've always got to put a spin on design." The retro look, she said, "pays homage to one of my favorite designers, Charles Anderson." In its vintage guise, and despite the rationale, it continues to have a curious allure. Maybe it's the recycled paper stock on which it was originally silkscreened.

print

America's Graphic Design Magazine

$8.00 US • $11.25 Canada • Print July/August 2003 LVII:IV

Gregory Crewdson (cover photography; from the *Dream House* series, Untitled 24-by-40-inch digital chromogenic print, 2001. Courtesy of Luhring Augustine Gallery, New York, and the artist)

Steven Brower (creative director)

This detail of a staged tableau by photographer Gregory Crewdson was part of the lead story about his imagery, which hinted "at the mystery and tension beneath the surface of middle-class America." Crewdson mastered an art of making cinematic frozen moments of suburban facades, with characters staring blankly at mysterious lights emerging from hidden places. As writer Peter Hall noted, these photographs presented "the everyday [as] under threat." This cover begged the question: What was the root of this anxious despair?

print

America's Graphic Design Magazine

FORMATTING THE NEWS
CALL-GIRL ADVERTISING
ALVIN LUSTIG'S LEGACY
KNIFE-EDGE MOTION GRAPHICS
BRANDED BUDGET AIRLINES
BRAZIL'S ARTFUL STREET POEMS

$10 US • $13 Canada • Print January/February 2004 LVIII:I

Print LVIII:I, January/February 2004

Paula Scher (cover artist)

Steven Brower (creative director)

Paula Scher's expressive scratches and scrawls on this cover introduced her graphic commentary "First Person: All The News That Fits," a critique of contemporary news coverage. "The tone and tenor of the news stays pretty much the same, regardless of the significance of the event," the editors noted. This was Scher's unique visual diary, annotated through her signature handlettering of the day's headlines.

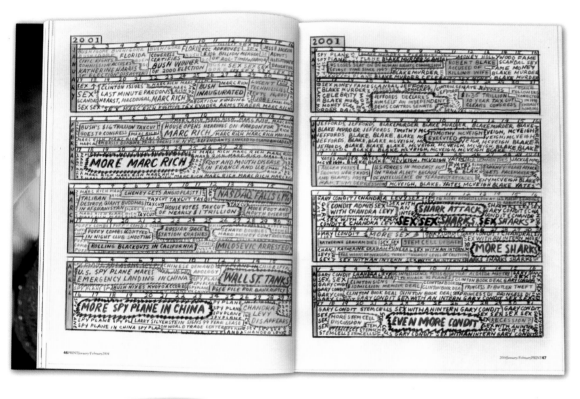

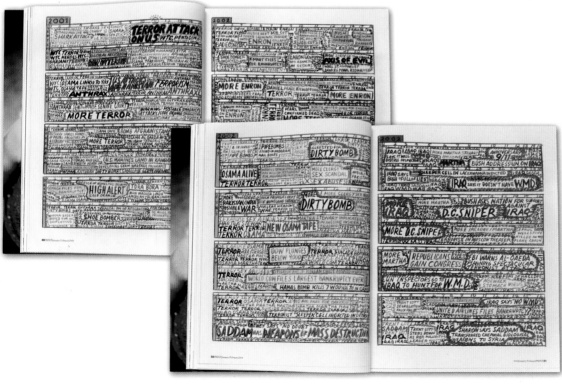

print

America's Graphic Design Magazine

sex issue

DESIGNING PORNOTOPIA

KINKY MUSEUMS

DIRTY COMICS

PIXEL VIXENS

$10 US • $13 Canada • Print July/August 2004 LVIII:IV

Print LVIII:IV, July/August 2004

Why Not Associates (cover design)

Bird Studios, London (cover 3D modeling)

Steven Brower (creative director)

T he original packaging for *Print*'s first (but not last) Sex Issue was wrapped in brown paper, as was once done with *Playboy, Penthouse* and other sensually sensitive, adults-only publications. The wrapper was part of the conceit that Why Not Associates devised, but it also served as both enticement and protection. Although nothing overtly prurient could be seen on the cover, the suggestive lettering in epidermal pink, created as a 3D illusion, had a curiously stimulating eroticism. As with almost all of *Print*'s controversial coverage, the Sex Issue was definitely hot among designers, yet the theme received mixed reviews from readers.

print

DESIGN CULTURE EARTH
JULY/AUGUST 2005 US$10/CAN$15

108 PT
I WILL NOT

84 PT
I WILL NOT DE

60 PT
I WILL NOT DESTR

48 PT
I WILL NOT DESTROY T

36 PT
I WILL NOT DESTROY THE EARTH

24 PT
I WILL NOT DESTROY THE EARTH. I WILL NOT DE

Print LIX:IV, July/August 2005

Michael Ian Kaye (cover designer and cover photography)

Stephanie Skirvin (art director)

Michael Ian Kaye's cover for *Print*'s Design for Good/Good for Design issue featured a type specimen chart with the phrase "I Will Not Destroy The Earth" as the sample setting. In the editorial note, Joyce Rutter Kaye said, "Getting to the 'good stuff' about sustainability ... was our challenge in creating this issue, and the challenge of anyone endeavoring to become more deeply involved in environmentally and socially engaged design." She added, "On an individual level, designers are recognizing their unique ability to take the movement from its dowdy 1970s roots and into the mainstream." Another challenge was, and still is, making the idea of conscience ring true in a field that is first and foremost creating allure and desire.

print

▶▶▶ DESIGN CULTURE MOTION
SEP/OCT 2005 US$19.50/CAN$25

INTERACTING WITH THE THINGS THAT SURROUND YOU

TAKE THIS MAGAZINE, FOR EXAMPLE—YOU COULD EAT IT, YOU COULD ROLL IT UP, YOU COULD STAND ON IT, YOU COULD EVEN READ IT. BUT WHY READ IT THE WAY YOU ALWAYS DO? JUST LEAVE THIS MAGAZINE IN THE FREEZER OVERNIGHT FOR A WHOLE NEW EXPERIENCE—A COLD, CRISP MAGAZINE WILL AWAIT YOU IN THE MORNING.* DON'T JUST THINK ABOUT IT, DO IT. YOU'LL BE VERY SURPRISED! LOOK, FEEL, SMELL, RUB GENTLY, PUT IT AGAINST YOUR CHEEK...THE MAGAZINE CHANGED OVERNIGHT. AND YOU CAN DO IT AGAIN AND AGAIN. FINALLY, PLEASE COMPLETE THE FOLLOWING SENTENCE: PRINT IS A _____ MAGAZINE.

SOME RANDOM POSSIBLE INTERACTIONS:

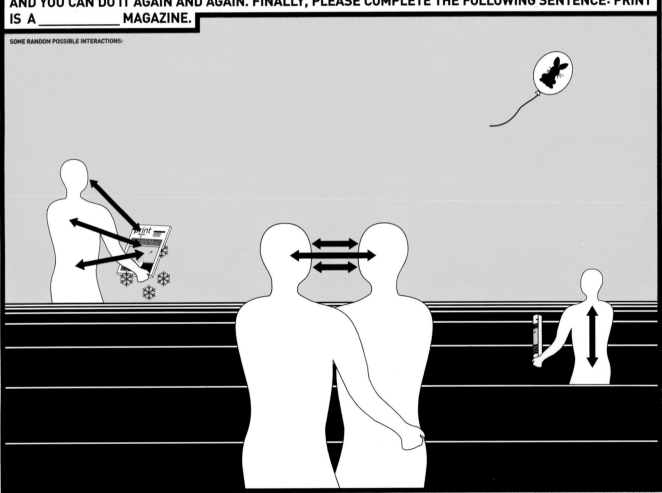

* COLD DOESN'T NECESSARILY MEAN COOL, AND VICE VERSA.

Print LIX:V, September/October 2005

karlssonwilker inc. (cover art)

Stephanie Skirvin (art director)

Art director Stephanie Skirvin called upon the masters of meta-concept design to comment on interactive design, the subject of this issue. With its typical wry irony, karlssonwilker responded with a mock infographic/how-to explaining the interactive options afforded the reader of "this magazine, for example," including rolling it up, standing on it, even reading it. This was illustrative of how *Print* was finding its way in the new digital space with its own point of view.

print

DESIGN CULTURE WORLD
JANUARY/FEBRUARY 2007

Global Dialogues 2007

Europe Versus Immigration

Berlin's New Direction

Banksy (Almost) Uncovered

Print LXI:I, January/February 2007

Cyan (cover art)

Kristina DiMatteo (art director)

When used as graphic elements, quotation marks, exclamation points, apostrophes and arrows are the comfort foods of graphic design. They say a little or a lot but do not overtax the brain. For *Print*'s Global Dialogues issue, Berlin-based Cyan illustrated the design conversation transpiring around the world and turned it into this cover. When reduced to their fundamental elements, despite the many languages and alphabets, graphic design and typographic design are indeed universal activities.

print

DESIGN CULTURE PLACE
JUNE 2008

The Art of European Design

Scotland's Tarted-Up Tartan
Iceland's Adorable Edge
Turkey's Controversial Cartoonists
France's Sexy Exhibitions

Print LXII:III, June 2008

Christoph Niemann (cover illustrator)

Kristina DiMatteo (art director)

---

*P*rint has had a few enigmatic and downright perplexing covers in its lifetime. Among the most beguiling was one by visual punster Christoph Niemann. When asked almost a decade after publication what these puzzling symbols meant, he replied, "I have to admit that I'm just as puzzled." But he nonetheless offered the following explanation: "Keyhole: conceptual illustration. Pencils: surface design. Game: interactive design. CD-ROM: interactive/animated projects on CDs (that was that time when those existed ... right?)."

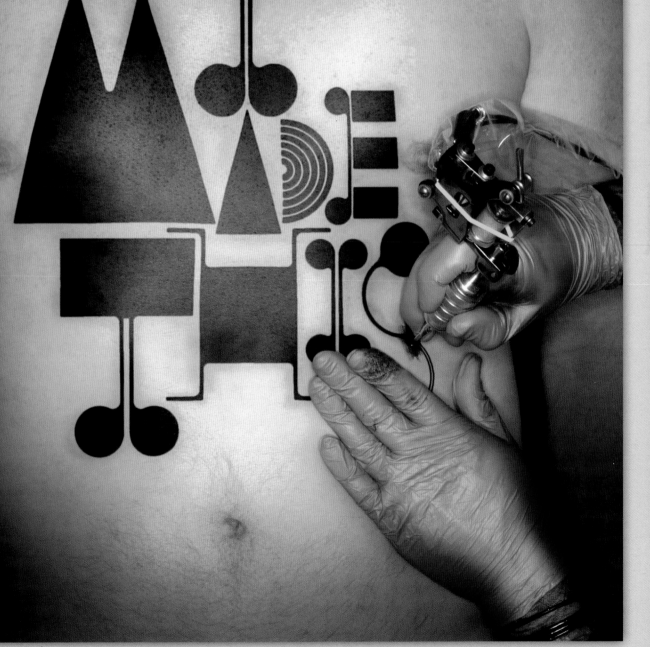

DESIGN FOR CURIOUS MINDS / OCTOBER 2009

THE UPS & DOWNS OF GOING GREEN / SCISSORHANDS: CUT-PAPER MANIACS /
CREATIVITY & COMMERCE WINNERS / LIFE INSIDE THE TARGET BULLSEYE

print

DECLARATIONS OF INDEPENDENCE

Exhibitionism with a conscience,
DIY gone digital, and 35
other trends from a wild and
contradictory decade.

Print LXIII:V, October 2009

Non-Format (cover art)
Darrell Eager (cover photography)
Alice Cho (art director)

Nearing the end of 2009 meant enough time had passed to assess the history of the graphic design field during that fin de siècle period from 1999–2009. Colin Berry wrote the following in his cover story: "It was a decade of contradictions: Authentic self-expression and self-absorbed foolishness coexisted, rebellion and well-honed skill established an uneasy harmony, and both the individual and collective instincts flourished." It was a period without a period style. Yet it was dominated by real and faux DIY techniques. This cover declared "I Made This" as the mantra of millennial design. *Print* called it "exhibitionism with a conscience."

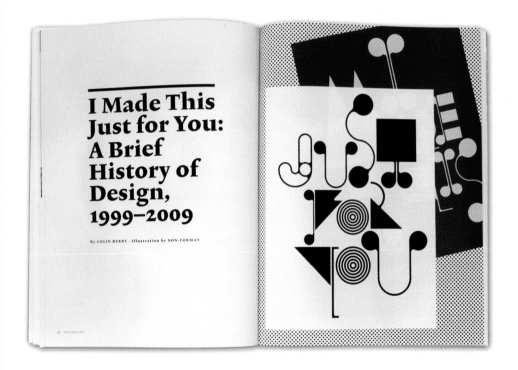

DESIGN FOR CURIOUS MINDS / JUNE 2010

GLASER / SCHER / KALMAN / CHEUK / FELLA / VANDERLANS / NIEMANN
VALICENTI / HORT / CHWAST / DOYLE / McFETRIDGE / LUPTON / + MORE

print

30 DESIGN SUPERSTARS

*Who has the power
and who's on the way up?*

Milton Glaser

Print LXIV:III, June 2010

Milton Glaser (cover artist)

Alice Cho (art director)

With the web usurping the role of many magazines, the paper version of *Print* had to find its *raison d'être*—and its own millennial voice. A new generation of editors (for this issue, Aaron Kenedi was editor-in-chief) engaged a stable of young and old writers and commissioned young and old designers to fill the issue with imagery that crossed generational divides. To illustrate the theme of 30 Design Superstars, Milton Glaser produced an image suggesting both E.T. and the Sistine Chapel yet not bound to any particular age or age group, while at the same time implying a passing of the proverbial torch.

DESIGN FOR CURIOUS MINDS / AUGUST 2010

EXCLUSIVE: ORIGINAL ART AND STRONG OPINIONS FROM ART CHANTRY, JOE DUFFY, MICHAEL IAN KAYE, SAGI HAVIV, BARBARA GLAUBER + MORE

print

11 designers have their say →

RANTS + RAVES

Print LXIV:IV, August 2010

James Victore (cover designer)

Tom Schierlitz (cover photography)

Kevin Demaria (art director)

This demonic-looking cudgel appeared to say more than the thousands of words and numerous pictures inside the Rants + Raves issue. James Victore's take-no-prisoners approach to graphic statements is arguably one of *Print*'s more strident covers both for its message and form. The content included more raves than rants, with one of the most complex yet hilariously strident of the latter being Felix Sockwell's "Felixbook" page on what's terribly wrong with the world for which design is partly responsible.

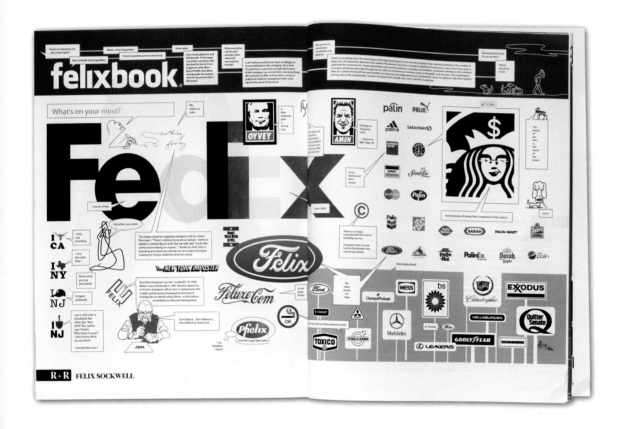

PRINT

SURPRISE ISSUE

REDEFINING DESIGN 65.3 JUNE 2011

HIDDEN
DESIGN
INSIDE

**YOUR BRAIN AT
WORK AND PLAY**

**DESIGN BY
CHANCE**

**THE NORDIC FOOD
REVOLUTION**

**THE HAND DRAWN
COMPETITION
WINNERS**

**YVES BÉHAR
LIGHTS A FUSE**

and edited by: Special section guest Designed
Kokoro
et
Moi.

Image Not Available

To see alternate covers visit

www
kokoro
moi
com

printcover

www.kokoromoi.com/printcover

Print 65.3, June 2011

Kokoro & Moi (cover art)

Tonya Douraghy (art director)

---

*P**rint*'s Surprise Issue may have been a surprise even to its editors. "This issue is an experiment," wrote executive editor Judy Grover. Calling attention to Kokoro & Moi's cover, art director Tonya Douraghy wrote, "They say you don't have a magazine until you have a cover. It's intriguing, then, that our Surprise Issue should have myriad digital covers. ... Kokoro & Moi's playful take on Web 1.0, revamped as printed matter, gives expression to our theme as a clever (but not too clever) package of anti-design." Kokoro & Moi also designed a special surprise interior section.

The Occupy Artist of Paris 1968 BY WILLIAM BOSTWICK

RICK POYNOR: DO DESIGNERS ACTUALLY HAVE ANY INFLUENCE? | IN THE STUDIO WITH OLIMPIA ZAGNOLI, PLUS LULZ WITH JENNIFER DANIEL

PRINT

REDEFINING DESIGN 66.1 FEBRUARY 2012

RIOT GRRRLS TAKE OVER THE LIBRARY
by Margaret Eby

SACRIFICING DESIGN'S SACRED COWS
by Alexandra Lange

SMALL-TOWN POLITICKING IN THE AGE OF OBAMA
by Fritz Swanson

THE POWER ISSUE

Print 66.1, February 2012

Mirko Ilić (cover artist)

Ben King (art director)

For the cover of The Power Issue, Mirko Ilić created an illustration that could be described as either "people power" or "mob power." The individuals comprising the upward-thrusting arrow are either moving in tandem with a shared belief or being forced to move as a compliant mass of believers. Articles in this issue covered different manifestations of power, such as the power of negativity, signs of authority, and expertise as a driver of power.

True Tales from Top Creatives   7 Compelling New Book Cover Designs

How to Reveal an Authentic Brand Story   Propaganda: The Art of Lying

PRINT

PRINTMAG.COM 67.5 OCTOBER 2013

DESIGN and STORYTELLING

Print 67.5, October 2013

Wendy MacNaughton (cover artist)

Ronson Slagle (art director)

What symbol evokes the idea of storytelling? In some quarters, catching the extra-big fish is the definition of the tall tale—which was the key to San Francisco artist Wendy MacNaughton's illustration for *Print*'s Design and Storytelling issue. "A great story is the heart and soul of all outstanding graphic design work," wrote editor Sarah Whitman in the editorial note. "An authentic narrative is what sets a brand apart from its competitors, even making it beloved." During the 2010s, graphic design became synonymous with a good story, and this issue focused on that quality in everything from brands to propaganda.

PRINT IS

PRINTMAG.COM 67.6 DECEMBER 2013

NOT DEAD
PRINT IS
NOT DEAD
PRINT IS
NOT DEAD

THE 2013
RDA IS
NOW HERE

Print 67.6, December 2013

Debbie Millman (cover designer)

Brent Taylor (photographer)

Ronson Slagle (art director)

D ebbie Millman, host of the popular online radio show "Design Matters," is part of the art/text designer as author movement that emerged in the 2000s. Her cover for *Print*'s 2013 Regional Design Annual was based upon a common mantra among traditional readers, viewers and designers. It suggested that either *Print* was still alive and publishing or that print as a form had a long way to go before it would be subsumed by the digital wave. Whatever the rationale, the artwork was a graphic design sampler for the 21st century.

PRINT

Why XXX is So Sultry

SEX and GRAPHIC DESIGN

Female Creatives Break Through the Glass Ceiling

Pin-ups, Pulps and Paperbacks

An Uncensored Look at Banned Comics

Print 68.1, February 2014

Rodrigo Corral, Devin Washburn (cover designers)

Ronson Slagle (art director)

For *Print*'s second issue devoted to sex, the inflated gold 'X' with its subtle reflection was an elegantly inoffensive way to state the theme without illustrating it in either a hardcore or softcore way. Nonetheless, 'X' is arguably the sexiest letter in the alphabet—think of two people and four legs intertwined—and certainly one of the most symbolically diverse. 'X' is the sign of a kiss in "XOXO." Add a couple more 'X's and 'XXX' is the universal symbol for "caution: adults only."

Conceive, Make, Sell — 28 Bold and Brilliant Design Entrepreneurs
Pixels Evolved: The 1980s Strike Back | Designers as Tomorrow's Leaders

PRINT

PRINTMAG.COM 68.3 JUNE 2014

THE INNOVATION ISSUE

Print 68.3, June 2014

Laura Bifano (cover designer)

Ronson Slagle (art director)

To make a stunning illustration for The Innovation Issue demanded a certain level of, well, innovation. What better than to dip into the past—not just the recent past, but the prehistoric one. For a symbolic tour de force, Laura Bifano's cover comically sums up the essence of innovation: vision beyond the norm. That *Print*'s caveman wields these tools also suggests innovative thinking because the average prehistoric hominoid was not known for nuanced chiseling.

From Chisel to Galaxie Polaris Heavy

T hough many versions of *Print*'s nameplate have appeared over the years, the covers did, at times, exhibit consistency. Detailed below are the five main logos used throughout *Print*'s history.

Print

1955-1960

Print

1960-1999

print

2000-2005

print

2005-2010

PRINT

2011-present